W9-ADL-583

Michelangelo

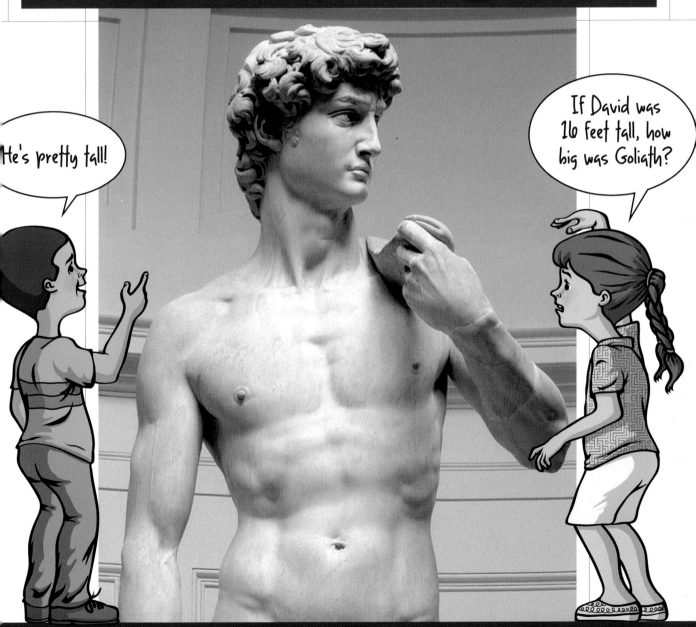

BY DARICE BAILER • ILLUSTRATED BY J.T. MORROW

The
Child's
World®

Published by The Child's World®
1980 Lookout Drive • Mankato, MN 56003-1705
800-599-READ • www.childsworld.com

Acknowledgments
The Child's World®: Mary Berendes, Publishing Director
Red Line Editorial: Editorial direction and production
The Design Lab: Design

Photographs ©: Arte & Immagini srl/Corbis, cover, 1, 17;
Nickolay Vinokurov/Shutterstock Images, 4; Georgios Kollidas/
Shutterstock Images, 5; Shutterstock Images, 6, 14; Domenico
Ghirlandaio, 9; Bryan Busovicki/Shutterstock Images, 12–13,
23; Malgorzata Kistryn/Shutterstock Images, 16; Michelangelo,
19; Walter McBride/Corbis, 20

Design Elements: Zern Liew/Shutterstock Images

ISBN 9781626873520
LCCN 2014930691

Printed in the United States of America
Mankato, MN
July, 2014
PA02223

ABOUT THE AUTHOR

Darice Bailer is the author of many books for young readers. She has won a Parents' Choice Gold Award and a Parents' Choice Approved Seal for her work.

ABOUT THE ILLUSTRATOR

J.T. Morrow has worked as a freelance illustrator for more than 25 years and has won several awards. His work has appeared in advertisements, on packaging, in magazines, and in books. He lives near San Francisco, California, with his wife and daughter.

CONTENTS

CHAPTER 1

The Young Artist

It was time for school. But seven-year-old Michelangelo wasn't listening. He was busy drawing pictures instead. And he couldn't stop. He drew on paper. He even drew on walls. He wanted to be an artist. Michelangelo lived in Florence, Italy. Florence was a busy place. This was the **Renaissance**. There were painters and sculptors hard at work. Michelangelo would grow up to become one of these great artists.

RENAISSANCE
Renaissance means rebirth. *It was a time period of great learning in art and science. The Renaissance began in Italy in the 1300s. It spread through Europe. Artists, writers, and scientists experimented with new ways of thinking and creating art.*

The Basilica of Saint Mary of the Flower, or the Florence Cathedral, was finished in Michelangelo's time and still stands in Florence today.

*Michelangelo grew up to become one of the greatest
artists of the Renaissance and of all time.*

When Michelangelo walked to school, he could see sculptors at work in their shops. Sculptors sculpted with blocks of stone. They gathered the stone from nearby mountains. They used the stone to make fireplaces or **sculptures**. Sculpting was loud and messy work. Michelangelo watched the sculptors bang their sharp **chisels** into hard stone. Michelangelo could see the sculptors creating figures. They hammered away and turned the stone into the shape of a person.

Tools have changed over time, but sculptors still use a hammer to hit a chisel, which breaks away and shapes the stone.

Michelangelo enjoyed art from a young age. He was always busy drawing. He soon started studying painting and sculpting. As he grew up, creating art became his life. He painted, sculpted, and designed famous churches. He created his own **masterpieces**. Today, Michelangelo is so famous that he is known by only his first name. Even hundreds of years after his time, people from around the world come to Italy to see his sculptures and paintings.

CHAPTER 2

Studying Art

Michelangelo Buonarroti was born in 1475 in Caprese, Italy. There is a legend that his mother fell off a horse while she was pregnant. She and the baby could have died. It was a miracle that they lived. Michelangelo's father was a religious man. So he and his wife called their baby boy Michelangelo. It comes from the name of an angel.

When Michelangelo was a baby, his parents moved to Florence. His family attended church. They read the Bible often. Michelangelo heard the stories of Noah's Ark and God's creation of man and Earth. Michelangelo would remember these stories when he grew up.

When Michelangelo was six, his mother died. His father took care of him. He sent Michelangelo to school a year later. Michelangelo's father hoped that his son would become a businessman. But Michelangelo only wanted to draw. His father couldn't talk him out of it. So he made sure his son studied with the most famous painter in Italy. This painter was Domenico Ghirlandaio.

Michelangelo learned about painting from Ghirlandaio. Ghirlandaio had a great skill for detail, as seen in his painting St. Jerome in His Study.

Ghirlandaio and his brother had a workshop. They invited young artists to study painting with them. At age 13, Michelangelo began working for the brothers. He was a painting **apprentice**. Michelangelo quickly showed his talent. He would look at a picture that had been drawn by a famous artist. Then he would draw it himself. It was hard to tell which drawing was the artist's and which was Michelangelo's.

One morning when Michelangelo was about 14 years old, he and a friend passed by a palace. A rich man named Lorenzo de Medici lived there. Lorenzo's palace had a garden filled with beautiful statues. Lorenzo invited young artists to study sculptures there. That day, the two boys saw a student making a clay sculpture. Michelangelo studied it.

Michelangelo borrowed some tools. Then he tried to copy one of the sculptures in the garden himself. As Michelangelo polished his first marble sculpture, Lorenzo watched. Michelangelo was very talented. Lorenzo invited him to live in his palace. There, he could practice sculpting.

MARBLE VERSUS CLAY

*Renaissance sculptors sometimes worked with clay. But they often liked to work with **marble** instead. Marble was hard as rock. Sculptors could polish marble so it looked shiny. The statues seemed to last forever. Clay was soft. Sculptors could shape it with their fingers. They could also add more clay to cover up a mistake. But clay broke more easily. It also couldn't be polished.*

CHAPTER 3

A Giant Statue

Word of Michelangelo's great talent began to spread throughout Italy. He was becoming famous. In 1498, a Catholic church leader asked Michelangelo to carve a beautiful statue. It was to be a pietà. Pietà is a Latin word. It means pity. A pietà is a sculpture of the biblical figure Mary cradling her son, Jesus.

So Michelangelo went into the mountains to find a good block of marble. He hauled the marble down the mountain on a wooden sled. Dust flew as Michelangelo hammered away with his chisel. He didn't wash for days. He ate very little. He wanted only to create something beautiful.

Michelangelo carved folds in Mary's dress. Her dress began to look real. He also carved sadness into Mary's eyes. And he showed a mother's love. In the middle of the Renaissance, Michelangelo did something new. He carved a mother's feelings into stone. When Michelangelo was done, it was one of the most beautiful sculptures in the world.

Michelangelo's Pietà *shows Mary's sadness after the death of her son, Jesus.*

Michelangelo's Pietà *can still be viewed inside St. Peter's Basilica in Vatican City in Rome.*

At first, people thought someone else sculpted Mary. So Michelangelo snuck into the church at night. He carved his name on Mary's dress. He wanted everyone to know he was the artist. He was only 25 years old.

After finishing the *Pietà*, Michelangelo began a new statue. There is a story in the Bible about a young boy named David. Using only a slingshot, David fights a giant named Goliath and wins. A cathedral in Florence wanted a statue of David to decorate the church. The church bought a giant piece of marble for the statue. This block of marble was 18 feet (5.5 m) tall. The job was huge. A sculptor began to chisel David, but he didn't do a good job. He only cut a little bit before leaving the block unfinished.

Now the giant block of marble was lying near the church. Could Michelangelo carve David? Michelangelo took the job in 1501. He started at the top with David's head. Locks of hair began to form. Next, Michelangelo chiseled out the face. There was determination in David's eyes. Michelangelo chipped away at the neck. He made it strong and thick.

REBIRTH OF ANCIENT TECHNIQUES

In ancient times, sculptors in Rome and Greece created statues that looked like real people. Then for hundreds of years, sculptors worked in different styles. During the Renaissance, artists began to look back on the Roman and Greek style of sculpting. Michelangelo studied ancient statues. He tried to create better ones. Michelangelo wanted to carve more than just a person's body. He wanted his marble figures to show feeling.

Michelangelo cut away another layer. He had studied bodies of people who had died. He knew what muscles, veins, and bones looked like. He used what he learned from studying bodies. He formed David's strong muscular arms. David's back, fingers, knees, and toes looked very real. Michelangelo shaped David's body all the way down to the toes. Finally, the tall lean body of David appeared on a **pedestal**. The year was 1504.

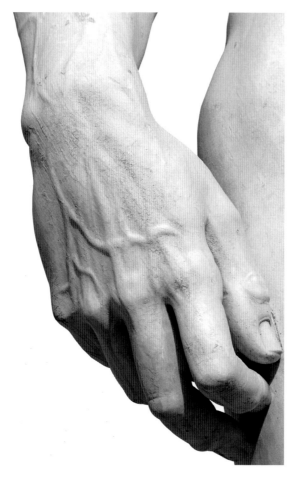

The giant marble figure was a masterpiece. It took 40 strong men to move it. Even though the statue was made of stone, Michelangelo showed David's courage. In the Bible, David bravely fought Goliath. Looking at the statue inspired the people of Florence to be brave. Michelangelo was now the greatest sculptor in Italy. Michelangelo's David is still the most famous statue in the world. Today you can see it in a museum in Florence.

Michelangelo's strict detail can be seen in David's *hands, which show veins, wrinkles, and fingernails.*

CHAPTER 4

The Artist Paints a Masterpiece

Four years passed. In 1508, the pope in Rome gave Michelangelo a new job. The pope wanted Michelangelo to paint the ceiling of the Sistine Chapel. The Sistine Chapel was a small church in Rome. The ceiling was 65 feet (20 m) high. The pope wanted Michelangelo to paint important people from the Bible.

FRESCOES

Many Renaissance painters painted **frescoes**. *The name* fresco *comes from an Italian word meaning* fresh. *Michelangelo ground up powder in water to make watercolor. He also mixed plaster out of water, lime, and sand. He spread the wet plaster. Then he quickly painted watercolor on top before it dried. When the plaster dried the painting became permanent.*

Michelangelo hadn't painted much since he was an apprentice. He preferred sculpting instead. But he needed money. His father was poor. He was counting on Michelangelo for help. So Michelangelo took the job. He started painting the Bible stories he knew best. He remembered the stories of God's creations from his childhood.

Michelangelo had sculpted people to look very real. Now he used a paintbrush to paint faces, arms, and toes as if he was sculpting them. The people he painted had shape, as if they were sculpted. He painted in watercolor frescoes.

One of the most famous Bible stories on the Sistine Chapel's ceiling is The Creation of Adam, *which shows God and Adam, the first man God created.*

Michelangelo barely ate. He barely slept. He worked day and night to finish the huge ceiling. Four years later, Michelangelo was done. The year was 1512. People in Rome flocked to see his work. He had painted 300 people on the ceiling! You can still see his famous work in the Sistine Chapel in Rome.

Michelangelo stood on a high platform and painted the entire ceiling while standing and looking up.

Michelangelo kept working throughout his life. When he was 75 years old, a new pope hired him. The pope asked Michelangelo to take over Saint Peter's Basilica in Rome. He wanted Michelangelo to be the head architect of the church. Michelangelo had been asked to design churches before. Whenever he did, he broke old rules of design. He made doors smaller, for example.

Michelangelo was getting old. He started drawing the dome of the new church. But he never lived to see it finished. Yet the dome and his art are still world famous. Millions of people come to see it. Michelangelo was a master of different art forms. People still admire his work. He is one of the greatest painters, sculptors, and architects of all time.

Glossary

apprentice (uh-PREN-tis) An apprentice is a person who learns a certain skill by working for an expert. When he was 13, Michelangelo became a painter's apprentice for Domenico Ghirlandaio and his brother.

chisels (CHIZ-uhlz) Chisels are tools with sharp ends that are used to cut and carve. Michelangelo used a hammer to bang his chisel into marble when sculpting.

frescoes (FRES-kohz) Frescoes are paintings made on wet plaster. Michelangelo's painting on the ceiling of the Sistine Chapel is a fresco.

marble (MAR-buhl) Marble is a hard, white stone that sometimes has colored patterns. Michelangelo collected his own marble from the mountains.

masterpieces (MAS-tur-pee-sez) Masterpieces are artworks of great excellence. Michelangelo's sculpture *David* is a masterpiece.

pedestal (PED-i-stuhl) A pedestal is a base or foundation on which something stands. Michelangelo's statue of David stands on a white pedestal.

Renaissance (REN-uh-sans) The Renaissance was a period of great learning in the arts and science between the 1300s and the 1600s. Leonardo da Vinci and Michelangelo were two of the greatest artists who lived during the Renaissance.

sculptures (SKUHLP-churz) Sculptures are objects that are carved and shaped out of stone, clay, wood, or other materials. Michelangelo liked making sculptures better than he liked painting.

To Learn More

BOOKS

Stanley, Diane. *Michelangelo*. New York: HarperCollins, 2003.

Sutcliffe, Jane. *Stone Giant: Michelangelo's David and How He Came to Be*.
Watertown, MA: Charlesbridge, 2014.

WEB SITES

Visit our Web site for links about Michelangelo:
childsworld.com/links

Note to Parents, Teachers, and Librarians:
We routinely verify our Web links to make sure they are safe and
active sites. So encourage your readers to check them out!

Index